Weather

Peter Riley
Consultant: Clive Carpenter

Miles Kelly PUBLISHING

First published in 2004 by
Miles Kelly Publishing Ltd
Bardfield Centre, Great Bardfield, Essex, CM7 4SL

Some material in this book can also be found in
100 Things You Should Know About Weather

Editor: Amanda Learmonth

Assistant Editor: Nicola Sail

Designer: Maya Currell

Indexer: Hilary Bird

British Library Cataloguing-in-Publication Data
A catalogue record for this book is available from the British Library

ISBN 1-84236-232-1

Printed in Singapore

www.mileskelly.net
info@mileskelly.net

ACKNOWLEDGEMENTS

The publishers would like to thank the following artists who have contributed
to this book:

Mark Bergin, Kuo Kang Chen, Steve Caldwell, Nicholas Forder, Chris Forsey, Terry Gabbey,
Shammi Ghale, Alan Hancocks, Alan Harris, Janos Marffy, Rachel Phillips, Martin Sanders,
Peter Sarson, Sarah Smith, Rudi Vizi, Steve Weston, Tony Wilkins

Computer-generated cartoons by James Evans

Contents

What is weather?

Rain, sunshine, snow and storms are all types of weather. Weather affects how we live, and how animals and plants survive. Different types of weather are caused by what is happening in the atmosphere, the air above our heads.

In parts of the world, the weather changes daily, in others, it is nearly always the same.

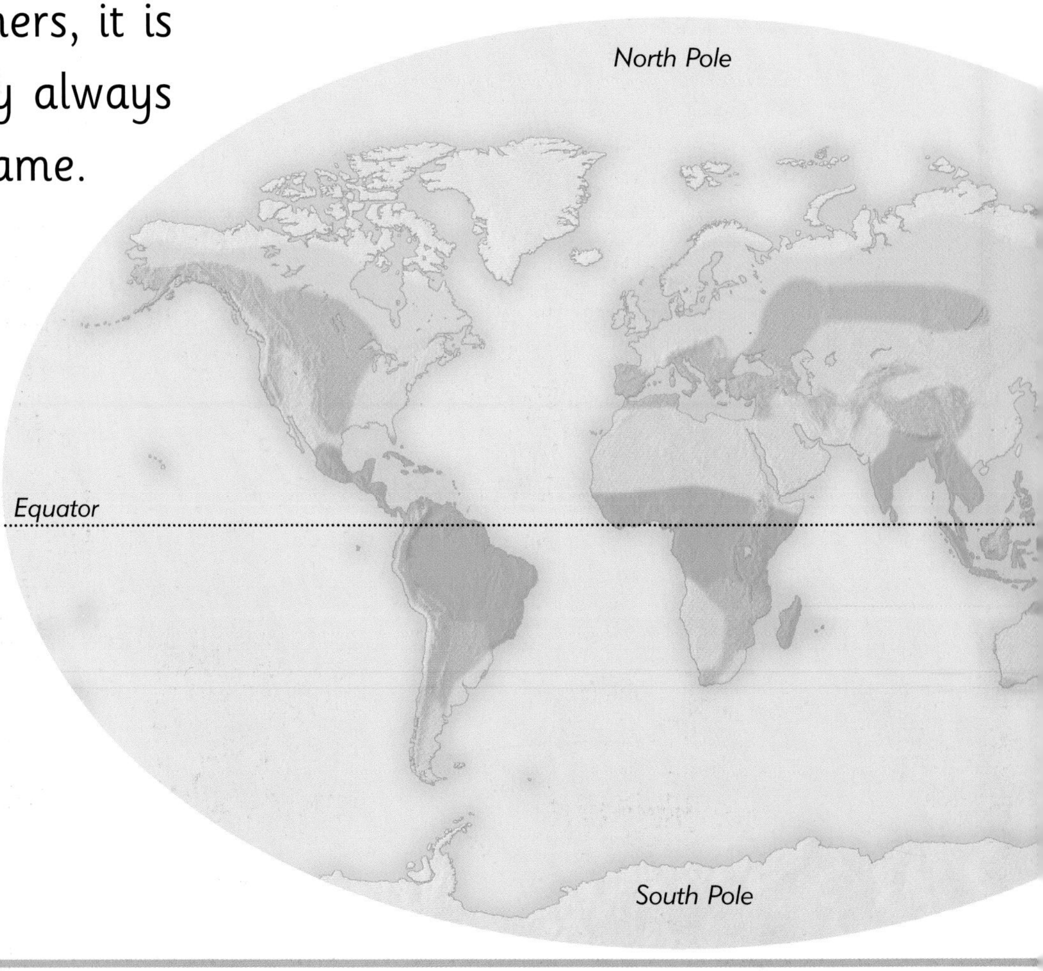

North Pole

Equator

South Pole

▼ *Use the coloured rings around the pictures below to match the different climate scenes to the main map.*

Most of the world has a temperate climate – it is neither too hot nor too cold.

Tropical

Cold temperate

Desert

Wet temperate

Near the North and South Poles, there is a cold, polar climate.

Mountainous

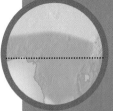

The Equator is an imaginary line around the middle of the Earth.

Dry temperate

Polar

5

All the seasons

The reason for the seasons lies in space.
Our planet Earth plots a path through space that takes it around the Sun. This path, or orbit, takes one year. The Earth is tilted, so over the year first one and then the other Pole leans towards the Sun, giving us seasons.

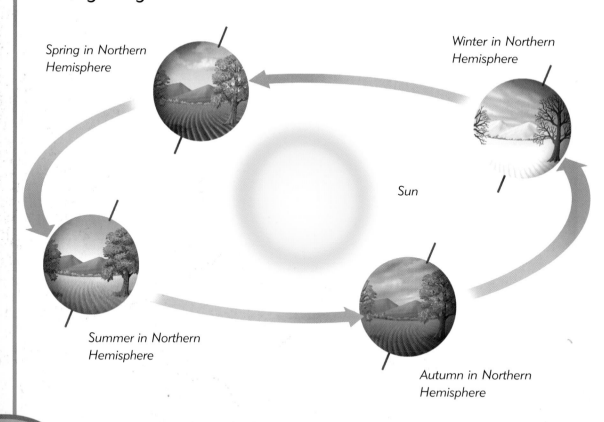

Spring in Northern Hemisphere

Winter in Northern Hemisphere

Sun

Summer in Northern Hemisphere

Autumn in Northern Hemisphere

▲ In June in the Northern Hemisphere, the North Pole leans towards the Sun. The Sun heats the northern half of the Earth and there is summer.

▲ At the North Pole during the height of summer, the Sun never disappears below the horizon.

▼ Many forests change colour in autumn. Trees prepare for the winter months ahead by losing their leaves. First, though, they suck back the precious green chlorophyll, or dye, in their leaves. This makes them turn glorious golden colours.

Summer in the Northern Hemisphere is between June and September.

Winter in the Northern Hemisphere is between December and March.

Sidney's fun facts!

In Stockholm, Sweden, the longest day lasts 21 hours because the Sun disappears below the horizon for only three hours!

Tropical seasons

Many parts of the tropics have two seasons, not four. The tropics are the parts of the world closest to the Equator. In June, tropical areas north of the Equator have the strongest heat and heaviest rains. In December, it is the turn of the areas south of the Equator.

◄ Rainforests have rainy weather all year round – but there is still a wet and dry season. It is just that the wet season is even wetter!

▼ Monsoons are winds that carry heavy rains. The rains fall in the tropics during the hot, rainy season. They can cause chaos, turning streets to rivers and even washing people's homes away.

Daily rainfall feeds the lush rainforest vegetation.

The tropics are always hot, as they are constantly facing the Sun.

▼ The tropics (shown here in red) lie either side of the Equator, between lines of latitude called the Tropic of Cancer and the Tropic of Capricorn.

Tropic of Cancer

Equator

Tropic of Capricorn

Sidney's fun facts!

In parts of monsoon India, over 26,000 millimetres of rain have fallen in a single year!

Scorching Sun

All our heat comes from the Sun. The Sun is a star, a super-hot ball of burning gases. It gives off heat rays that travel 150 million kilometres through space to our planet. Over the journey, the rays cool down, but they can still scorch the Earth.

▶ The Sahara Desert is the sunniest place on Earth. It is home to people such as the Tuareg Arabs.

Test your memory!

1. How many seasons are there in the tropics?
2. What is the name of the imaginary line that runs around the middle of the Earth?
3. What kind of climate will you find in the North Pole?

1. two 2. the Equator 3. a cold, polar climate

▶ Too much sun brings drought. Without rain, crops die and people and their animals go hungry.

Desert peoples cover their heads to protect them from the hot sun and sand.

Camels have long eyelashes to keep sand out of their eyes.

Strong winds blow the dry earth causing dust storms.

11

Layers of air

Our planet is wrapped in a blanket of air.
We call this blanket the atmosphere. It stretches hundreds of kilometres above our heads. The blanket keeps in heat, especially at night when part of the planet faces away from the Sun. During the day, the blanket becomes a sunscreen instead. Without an atmosphere, there would be no weather.

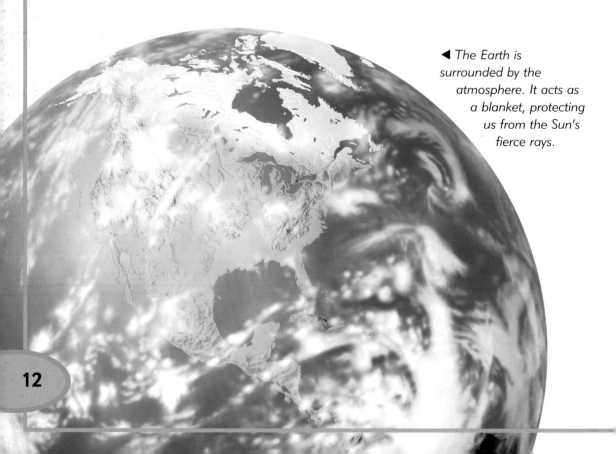

◄ *The Earth is surrounded by the atmosphere. It acts as a blanket, protecting us from the Sun's fierce rays.*

Exosphere
190 to 960 kilometres

Thermosphere
80 to 190 kilometres

Mesosphere
50 to 80 kilometres

Stratosphere
10 to 50 kilometres

Troposphere
0 to 10 kilometres

Low-level satellites orbit within the outer layers of the atmosphere.

Meteorites, pieces of rock from space, burn up in the atmosphere.

Mountaineers wear masks that help them breathe in more oxygen.

▲ The higher up you go, the less oxygen there is in the air. We need oxygen to breathe, so mountaineers often wear special breathing equipment.

◄ The atmosphere stretches right into space. Scientists have split it into five layers, or spheres, such as the troposphere.

Clouds and rain

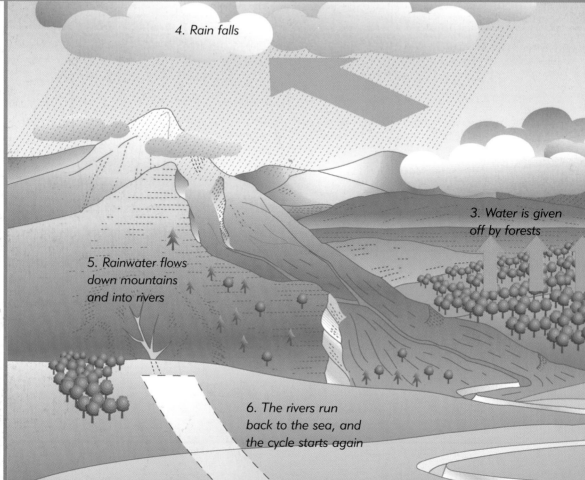

4. Rain falls

3. Water is given off by forests

5. Rainwater flows down mountains and into rivers

6. The rivers run back to the sea, and the cycle starts again

Rain comes from the sea. As the Sun heats the ocean's surface, some seawater turns into water vapour (a kind of gas) and rises into the air to form clouds. Rain falls from the clouds, some of which is soaked up by the land, but a lot finds its way back to the sea. This is the water cycle.

Make a rain gauge

You will need:
• jam jar • marker pen • ruler • notebook • pen

1. Place the jam jar where the rain can fall into it.
2. Use the marker pen to mark the water level on the outside of the jar.
3. Keep a record of the changing levels in a notebook.

Mountains can be so tall that their peaks are hidden by cloud.

2. Clouds form

Rain is made from lots of water droplets.

1. Water evaporates (disappears into the air) from the sea

Clouds gobble up heat, making it feel warmer.

15

Lots of clouds

Clouds come in all shapes and sizes. To help recognize them, scientists split them into ten basic types. The type depends on what the cloud looks like and where it forms in the sky. Cirrus clouds, for example, look like wisps of smoke. They form high in the troposphere and rarely mean rain.

▶ *The main classes of cloud – cirrus, cumulus and stratus – were named in the 1800s. A British weather scientist called Luke Howard identified the different types.*

Cumulonimbus clouds give heavy rain showers

Cumulus clouds bring rain

16

Mix and match

Can you match the names of these five types of clouds to their meanings?

1. Altostratus
2. Cirrus
3. Cumulonimbus
4. Cumulus
5. Stratus

a. heap
b. layer
c. high + layer
d. wisp
e. heap + rain

1. c 2. d 3. e 4. a 5. b

Cirrostratus, or mackerel skies, are usually a sign of changeable weather

Stratus clouds can bring drizzle or appear as fog

Contrails are the white streaks made by planes.

Cirrus clouds appear at great heights from the ground.

Mackerel skies are so-called because they look like fish scales.

17

Too much rain

Too much rain brings floods. There are two different types of floods. Flash floods happen after a short burst of heavy rainfall, usually caused by thunderstorms. Broadscale flooding happens when rain falls over a wide area – for weeks or months – without stopping. When this happens, rivers slowly fill and then burst their banks. Tropical storms, such as hurricanes, can also lead to broadscale flooding.

▲ *Flooding can cause great damage to buildings and the countryside.*

▲ When rain mixes with earth it makes mud, which can flood. On mountainsides there are no tree roots to hold soil together. An avalanche of mud can slide off the mountain.

Houses near rivers are at risk of being flooded out.

Mudslides can destroy whole towns and villages.

Desert flash floods can create streams of muddy brown water.

▲ There can be floods in a desert. When a lot of rain falls very quickly onto dry land, it cannot soak in. Instead it sits on the surface, causing flash floods.

19

Snow and ice

Snow is made of tiny ice crystals. When air temperatures are very cold – around zero degrees Celsius – the water droplets in the clouds freeze to make tiny ice crystals. Usually these clump together to form snowflakes. Most snowflakes look like six-pointed stars, but they come in other shapes too. No two snowflakes are the same.

▲ Falling snow is made worse by strong winds, which can form deep drifts.

Piles of ice form amazing shapes, like this arch.

▼ Antarctica, at the South Pole, is a frozen wilderness. Here, the weather never warms up enough for the ice to thaw.

▲ Avalanches happen after lots of snow falls on a mountain. The slightest movement or noise can jolt the snow and start it moving down the mountain.

An avalanche gathers speed as it thunders down the mountainside.

Sidney's fun facts!

Antarctica is the coldest place on Earth. Temperatures of –89.2 degrees Celsius have been recorded there.

Windy days

Wind is moving air. Winds blow because air is constantly moving from areas of high pressure to areas of low pressure. The bigger the difference in temperature between the two areas, the faster the wind blows.

◄ People can use the energy of the wind to make electricity for our homes. Tall turbines are positioned in windy spots. As the wind turns the turbine, the movement powers a generator and produces electrical energy.

▶ You can tell how windy it is by looking at the leaves and branches on a tree.

22

Force 0: Calm

Force 2: Light breeze

Force 3: Gentle breeze

Force 4: Moderate breeze

The Beaufort Scale is named after the Irish admiral who invented it.

Force 1: Light air

▶ Wind strength is measured on the Beaufort Scale. The scale ranges from Force 0, meaning total calm, to Force 12, which is a hurricane.

Force 5: Fresh breeze

Force 7: Near gale

Force 6: Strong breeze

Force 9: Strong gale

Trees can be forced into strange shapes by the wind.

Force 8: Gale

Force 10: Storm

A gale can rip the tiles off a roof.

Test your memory!

1. At what temperature does water freeze?
2. How many types of cloud are there?
3. Where does rainwater come from?

1. zero degrees Celsius **2.** seven **3.** the sea

Force 11: Violent storm

Force 12: Hurricane

Thunderclap!

Thunderstorms are most likely in summer. Hot weather creates warm, moist air that rises and forms tall cumulonimbus clouds. Inside each cloud, water droplets and ice crystals bang about, building up positive and negative electrical charges. Electricity flows between the charges, creating a flash that heats the air around it – this is lightning.

How close?

Lightning and thunder happen at the same time, but light travels faster than sound. Count the seconds between the flash and the clap and divide them by three. This is how many kilometres away the storm is.

Lightning that travels from the cloud to the ground is called fork lightning.

▼ *Hailstones are chunks of ice that fall from thunderclouds.*

Hailstones can be bigger than melons!

▲ *Lightning comes in different colours. If there is rain in the thundercloud, the lightning looks red. If there is hail, it looks blue.*

◄ *Lightning is so hot that it makes the air expand (spread out), making a loud noise or thunderclap.*

Dramatic flashes of lightning light up the sky.

25

Violent winds

Some winds travel at speeds of more than 120 kilometres an hour. Violent tropical storms happen when strong winds blow into an area of low pressure and start spinning very fast. They develop over warm seas and pick up speed until they reach land, where there is no more moist sea air to feed them. Such storms bring heavy rain.

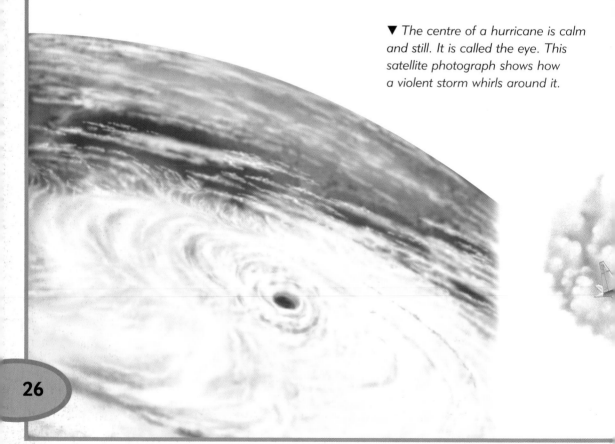

▼ The centre of a hurricane is calm and still. It is called the eye. This satellite photograph shows how a violent storm whirls around it.

Hurricane Hunter pilots do a risky job, but they help to save lives.

▲ As the hurricane races over the ocean, the winds create giant waves.

As the eye of the storm passes over, there is a pause in the wind and rain.

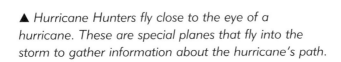

A hurricane destroys nearly everything in its path.

27

▲ Hurricane Hunters fly close to the eye of a hurricane. These are special planes that fly into the storm to gather information about the hurricane's path.

In a spin!

Tornadoes spin at speeds of 480 kilometres an hour! These whirling columns of wind are some of the most destructive storms on Earth. They form in strong thunderstorms, when the back part of the thundercloud starts spinning. The spinning air forms a funnel that reaches down towards the Earth. When it touches the ground, it becomes a tornado.

▶ A tornado can cause great damage to anything in its path.

Minneapolis

Sioux Falls

U. S. A.

Kansas City St Louis

Wichita

Amarillo Oklahoma City

Dallas

New Orleans

Houston

Mexico

Waterspouts are pillars of spinning water sucked up by a tornado.

Dust devils are desert tornadoes that create a whirling storm of sand.

▲ Hundreds of tornadoes happen in Tornado Alley, in the American Mid-West, shown in the shaded area.

Sidney's fun facts!

Waterspouts can suck up fish living in a lake!

Light shows

Rainbows are caused by sunlight passing through falling raindrops. The water acts like a prism (a triangle-shaped piece of glass), which splits the light. White light is made up of seven colours – red, orange, yellow, green, blue, indigo and violet – so these are the seven colours, from top to bottom, that make up a rainbow.

▲ Rainbows are most likely to be seen towards the end of the day, especially where thunderstorms build up during hot summer days.

▲ Some rainbows are just white. Fogbows happen when sunlight passes through a patch of fog. The water droplets are too small to work like prisms, so the arching bow is white or colourless.

A halo looks like a circle of light surrounding the Sun or Moon.

Mock suns are two bright spots that appear on either side of the Sun.

Auroras are curtains of lights in the sky. They are a dazzling light show!

Remember the rainbow!

Richard Of York Gave

Battle In Vain

The first letter of every word of this rhyme gives the first letter of each colour of the rainbow – as it appears in the sky:

Red Orange Yellow

Green Blue Indigo Violet

31

Made for deserts

Some animals have adapted to life in very hot, dry climates. Camels do not sweat until their body temperature hits 40 degrees Celsius, helping them to save water. Spadefoot toads stay underground in a cool burrow for most of the year.

Camel

Iguana

Banded gecko

Desert scramble!

Unscramble the letters to find the names of four kinds of animal that can cope with a very dry climate:

1. MELAC   **2.** ZILRAD
3. KOGEC   **4.** ODAT

1. CAMEL 2. LIZARD 3. GECKO 4. TOAD

Lizards do not need much water to survive in the dry desert.

A spadefoot toad only comes out of its burrow after rain.

◄▼ These animals live in different deserts around the world.

Spadefoot toad

Camels' humps contain fat stores for when there is little to eat or drink.

33

Weather clues

Long ago, people looked to nature for clues about the weather. One of the most famous pieces of weather lore goes like this: 'Red sky at night is the sailor's delight'. This means that a glorious sunset will be followed by a fine morning. There is no evidence that the saying is true, though.

▶ A blood-red sunset is delightful to look at, but, unfortunately, it cannot help a sailor to predict (accurately guess) the next day's weather.

Test your memory!

1. What is the centre of a hurricane called?
2. What is the name of the pillar of whirling water sucked up by a tornado?
3. How many colours of the rainbow are there?
4. What are white rainbows called?

1. the eye 2. a waterspout 3. seven 4. fogbows

Seaweed was once used as a way of telling if rain was on the way.

Groundhogs are said to tell the weather when they wake.

Weather records from ancient China were found scratched on this shell.

Guessing the weather

Working out what the weather will be like is called forecasting. By looking at changes in the atmosphere, and comparing them to weather patterns of the past, forecasters can make an accurate guess at what the weather will be tomorrow, the next day, or even further ahead. But even forecasters get it wrong sometimes!

A cold front (where cold air pushes under warm air) is shown by a blue triangle

A warm front (where warm air pushes over colder air) is shown by a red semi-circle

Black lines with red semi-circles and blue triangles are where a cold front meets a warm front

These white lines are isobars – closely spaced isobars mean strong wind

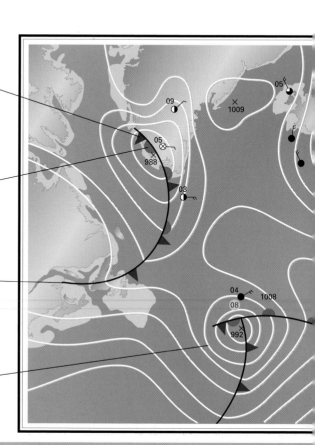

Weather symbols

Learn how to show the weather on your own synoptic charts. Here are some of the basic symbols to get you started. You may come across them in newspapers or while watching television. Can you guess what they mean?

A warm front is a sign of cooler weather to come.

A cold front can bring heavy rain and thunderstorms.

◀ Weather scientists, called meteorologists, plot their findings on maps called synoptic charts.

The white circle shows how much cloud cover there is

The three lines on the tail show that the wind is very strong

This shows an area of calm, with lots of cloud cover

Weather symbols make up a common language for meteorologists worldwide.

Watching the weather

Satellites help save lives. Their birds'-eye view of the Earth allows them to take amazing pictures of our weather systems. They can track hurricanes as they form over the oceans. Satellite-imaging has helped people to leave their homes and get out of a hurricane's path just in time.

◄ A weather satellite takes photographs of the Earth's weather systems in space.

Satellites take some of the best weather photographs.

◀ Weather balloons are hot-air balloons that are sent high into the atmosphere. Onboard equipment takes readings about the weather.

Weather balloons are used around the world every day.

Snoopy's long nose monitors the weather.

▲ Weather planes test the air ahead of the plane. This is *Snoopy*, one of the British weather planes.

39

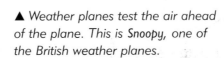

Index